I0764365

Sum Ledger

SUM LEDGER

by

Adam Tavel

Measure Press
Savannah, Georgia

Printed in the United States of America
First Edition

The text of this book is composed in Baskerville.
Composition by R.G.
Manufacturing by Ingram.

Tavel, Adam
Sum Ledger / by Adam Tavel — 1st ed.

ISBN-13: 978-1-939574-35-0
ISBN-10: 1-939574-35-8
Library of Congress Control Number: 2023941721

JACKET ART: *Deflationary*
(2021)
by Madara Mason
Digital media.

Measure Press
2 Longberry Lane
Savannah, GA 31419
http://www.measurepress.com/measure/

Acknowledgements

Thanks are due to the editors of the following journals where these poems first appeared, sometimes in earlier versions:

American Literary Review
Arts & Letters
Big Muddy
The Boiler
Clackamas Literary Review
Copper Nickel
Crazyhorse
Dialogist
Gargoyle
Hawai'i Review
The Hollins Critic
The Henniker Review
Jet Fuel Review
Meridian
Mudlark
New Ohio Review
The Nottingham Review
The Offing
Parcel
Passages North
The Penn Review
Pleiades
Plume
Puerto del Sol
Quarter After Eight
Queen of Cups
Rappahannock Review
RipRap
Rise Up Review
Sierra Nevada Review
Sixth Finch
Spoon River Poetry Review
Sugar House Review
The Summerset Review
Sycamore Review
Tar River Poetry
The William & Mary Review
Yemassee

"Until the Beast Was Slain" and "The Devouring" both first appeared in *At Length*. Jonathan Farmer has my enduring gratitude for publishing these long poems.

I'm also grateful to William Hathaway, who first read these poems and whose insights proved invaluable. The greatest thanks are due to my family: Ann, James, Graham, and Roan.

for David Hillenburg

"I know of no country, indeed, where the love of money has taken stronger hold on the affections of men."

— Alexis De Tocqueville, 1835

CONTENTS

I.

Rolling Pennies

Uncorked, my platypus bank
splattered its guts across our table.
The paper tubes collapsed
on each new coin that wedged
diagonally until my pinky mashed
it flat. Had I read Thucydides
I would have said the mound
shimmered like a phalanx
of copper helmets waves
refused to drown or rinse
but heaped in tide pools
for the daft amusement of gulls
hopping among the rank
nebulae of brains, in search
of minnows. All I knew
at ten was that my mother
had one diaper left for twin
daughters, my sisters, dreaming
in mismatched bassinets
a story above us. A pot of bottles
cooled from boiling as she tiptoed
to the door, her van key knifing
through her fist. I knew her nod
meant that from my perch
by the window I could await
her return, prideless as a skull.

Ode to Trailer Parks

ratty little snot-nose, ratty little lark,
ratty little bug zapper's sizzle in the dark

ratty little tricycle, ratty little gnome,
ratty little star-glitz the strays stalk home

ratty little backboard, ratty little net,
ratty little sneaker-squeak and fist-bump bet

ratty little crabgrass, ratty little rain,
ratty little switchblade twirling in a drain

ratty little frog jar, ratty little creek,
ratty little squealers playing hide and seek

ratty little fly zone, ratty little roar,
ratty little symphony of slamming doors

ratty little district, ratty little dope,
ratty little tire pile where kittens mope

ratty little country, ratty little gleam,
ratty little lady with her torch gone green

ratty little land mass, ratty little seas,
ratty little frigates with their planks all squeezed

ratty little cloud ball, ratty little tons,
ratty little boomerang around the sun

ratty little black hole, ratty little hurl,
ratty little nebula with its rainbow swirl

ratty little maker, ratty little beard,
ratty little maestro with his charts all smeared

ratty little darkness, ratty little light,
ratty little encore on closing night

ratty little Ichabod, ratty little Jane,
ratty little hand-holds who share their name

ratty little trailer, ratty little drive,
ratty little babysitter paid in fives

ratty little cover-tuck, ratty little kiss,
ratty little fever the lips can't miss

ratty little whimper, ratty little cloth,
ratty little cuddle and a sip of broth

ratty little hush-shush, ratty little thrum,
ratty little ghosty notes that make us hum

The 1909 Maryland Field Phantoms of Lewis Wickes Hine, National Child Labor Committee Photographer

I.

Irvan Stevans, A Young Berry Picker for Farrand Packing Co. on Curran's Farm, Where He & Another Boy Were the Only Whites Working with a Large Number of Negroes & Bad Language Was Abundant

Fuck this mush-crop half rotted on the vine,
this field more sand than soil, old bossman sun
our redneck whipcrack honcho hunching us
between these prickly rows. Fuck the canners,
their fans that purr & lick at blocks of ice —
on stools there's shade enough to scheme & fuss
for union pay. Out here we stock the shelves
of Baltimore & snarl *I'll wreck your girl.*
By dusk all knees are blood & puss & fucking brown.

II.

Laura, a Nine-Year-Old Berry Picker on Rock Creek, Been Working in the South Two Winters

How many cents your picking sweat can grouse
is counted by the boxes at your feet,
obscured by the throat-high vine one fist peels
& ripping clean of fruit will let spring back
against your chin. Miraculous your blouse
sail-white, your feline nose, your widow's peak
where wispy bangs like pale anemone
waver weightless. Of course we cannot see
the stains sprayed up from fruit stomped by your heels.

III.

A Four-Year-Old Helper in the Berry Field, Rock Creek, Whose Mother Says "He Helps a Little"

Now every time he wears his father's hat
I see again my husband's face, though dead,
stone drunk & cut in half on trolley tracks.
Such hate in me for rye & the half-rotted
box-tray this whiner wastes a day to fill.
So much I loathe his phantom countenance
at night I shake & slap the sloth from him.
Goddamn the shilpit blood that makes him jerk
away from hands that quake their absolution work.

Until The Beast Was Slain

for residents of the Wicomico County Almshouse, 1871–1923

"I beheld until the beast was slain
and its body destroyed and given
to the blazing flame."
— *Daniel 7:11*

I.
Deemed

Every person within the confines
of Wicomico or Somerset Counties,
Maryland, not being insane,
who has no visible means of maintenance
from property or personal labor
or is not permanently supported
by his or her friends or relatives,
who lives idle, without employment,
& every person who leads
a dissolute or disorderly course
of life & cannot give account
of the means by which he or she procures
a legitimate livelihood, & every nomad,
gypsy, or other person practicing
that which is commonly called
fortune-telling by acts, signs, or omens,
for value or otherwise, or any common
gambler, shall be deemed a vagabond;
& every person who wanders
begging in the limits

of Wicomico or Somerset Counties
from house to house or sits or stands
or takes position in any place
or begs from passersby, either by words
or gestures, shall be deemed
a beggar; & every person who wanders
& lodges in outhouses, sheds,
marketplaces, barracks, barns
or in any public building or in the open air
& has no permanent place
of abode or visible means of maintenance
shall be deemed a vagrant.

II.
Preliminary

left there two   small frame
buildings   dilapidated
slave quarters   unsuccessfully
repurposed   rubble erect
leaned for these   dirt counties'
mad whelps   reluctantly
some pity funds   trickle
three colored   & a lone
white patient   my candids
two attendants sir   appearing
almost hostile   there is nothing
wherefore   the deranged
restrained   their countenances
toad-eyed   by my flash

III.
Canary

my cold hominy
between the bars for
Herbert Herbert yellow
because the kernels
his feathers like them
boy they say boy
you stare that bird down
is it your saint
so much for miracles
and then their fists
batter back stars
swirling I keel
whispering Herbert if
they hurt you Jesus
will rend heaven though
mama said no beasts
of air nor land nor sea nor
lilies spinning not
in glory is they arrayed

IV.
Wind

a hand   need not splay
near a sash nor   baseboard nor
cracked plaster gaps   one
can sit or   stand or
take position here   & know

the vicious   whip-rush
whoosh of wind   ripping
crusted meal-sack   blankets
off cots to   splay over
floorboards   stooping sir
despite   repugnancy I folded
one wants   an arsenal
of soap   the smears
of feces blood   & there
under one   a pile of teeth

V.
Cuffed

stink like dock dredge | like cabbage
boiled | July outhouse reeking these
teeth if teeth could grind the slop
my wrists | both them | gnaw them
& rub the stumps against my neck

VI.
Orderly

at night her moans to shrieking
sheered you must understand
feeble-minded like the rest
she had these fits her nails
opened forearms like gutted
shad she would lift
her gown & stroke herself

before us without
regard for shame or
propriety you cannot bring
the governor's little camera
to this remove pretending
that any goodly Christian
elsewhere would stand
the infernal odor or
the pussing scratches night
after goddamn night sir
some liberties I took I
I took until she hushed

VII.
Plummet

the deceased   left
bedded   one two days &
the swale skin   jading
a convenience   common
practice   for the undertaker
field gloves   stripping down
dawn   batty Margaret
ajar I witnessed   the window
her ruffle-rush   plummeting
from stories   up it is
difficult   to conceive sir
that anything   worse than
this state   exists

VIII.
Rash

behold abandonment
down seven country miles
a parched stalk nation

where irrigators flake
vermillion in September's
relentless drought obliterating

where razor grass weeps
over the concrete slab
& headstone skewed

roadside for the asylum
so long reclaimed by weeds
one could fist them out forever

until a rust-dusk blazes
up the spectered rash
its tyranny to deem

there the carriage-creased lane
there the drooped porch stoop
snaggletooth shingles slanting

& there the length of chain
kinked about the throat
of midnight gagging

Mayflower Bastard

I saw the coast emerge despite the fog.
Arrhythmic and abrupt, the shrieks of gulls
sent our deckhands scurrying to lean
into salt-spray. They made a row of Cs,

the muscles in their necks taut as hog-
hide. Beneath my feet I felt the hull's
strained planks groan. Dingy little sunbeams
mottled masts, my prayer book, these jaundiced

hands that split and bleed each night in greasy
pot-suds. For weeks I dreamt I threw my face
back at kerchiefs shooing us across the sea
and woke to molars wiggling loose. With haste

the mates struck up a song of London Town.
In all these dreams I knew that we would drown.

II.

A Kindergartner's Concise History of the United States

for Al Maginnes

When they got here the fields
weren't fields. Not even green
or big flat. They had to grow
all the trees inside themselves.
The one brown road led down
to the river. George Washington
was the first one born. He rode
his horse until they made him
president. It's hard to remember
the names of any presidents
who came after. The trees
they made climb tall here
and live as woods. One tree
can't be woods alone.
When it snows or doesn't
and all the winter cold comes
we take a piece, we take it
inside and watch it burn.

Elective

September 11, 2001

It's an ordinary story, how I left
the dining hall holding a bagel
and coffee, waiting for aspirin
to unthrob my hangover.
I looked up at a muted screen
to see the first plane

crumple like an old accordion.
The slow-mo clip replayed above
the meal plan clerk, absorbed
in her crossword. I had forgotten
my cream cheese. Professor Davis
passed by and said good morning.

What a terrible accident, I thought,
before remembering my part in class
and entering the theater early
groped for my prop pistol
in the backstage velvet darkness
where I rehearsed my lines.

Thanksgiving Chorus

Kindergarteners beautiful and dumb
beam on risers to sing the goofy words
their teacher drilled *ad nauseam* all week.
She stands before them now, her soundless mouth
stretching every syllable. No one holds
hand-cut cardboard muskets as I once did,

dressed in pilgrim black, lost in floodlight glare,
comforted that my flat and off-beat notes
were drowned by girls whose headdress feathers waved
at mothers blurred behind their Polaroids
that flashed and whirred before they spit out squares
of celluloid that froze our chubby grins.

I waited for my ride with yawning nuns
whose habits snapped the wind, fluttery
and aloof as crows, who lorded over me,
their final zealot on the sidewalk's edge
as I perfected the art of double knots
and roping frothy spit down drainage grates.

When no one came I shot November sky,
the playground swings and pregnant clouds
gone gray, and then, at last, the paneling
on my grandmother's Buick wagon.
But here, no capotain or leather fringe
demarcates the stage's tribes. A rainbow owl

arrays the brown-bag shirt my son adjusts
nervously beside his friends. Raised cell phones
record our grown-up voices belting out
the gobble-gobble song we've joined in late
before frantically we all press pause.
Our ovation cocoons us in applause.

Construction Paper Flags Tacked to a Primary School Bulletin Board

for my sons

This one has concentric frames
that on close inspection are
pink strips of floss. This one
swims inside itself, three shades
of blue. This one's stripes
are dead calligraphy: R.I.P. Abuela,
R.I.P. Cousin Juan. This one grows
bored and morphs into a sketch
of a cartoon baseball twirling
its handlebar mustache.
This one begs God Bless. This one
has sticker pistols flashing BANG.
This one's wrists wear broken chains.
This one is lost inside the glitz
of caked-on glitter gold. This one
is impasto red on red that bled
on everything it touched. This one
has forty macaroni stars
and this one has the husk
of a dragonfly where stars
should be, its glue-gobbed wings
unstitching from the corpse.

Smear

Brooding lunchless at a newsprint easel
I ran my hands over paint lids crusted shut.
Outside the rain-glossed pane I saw their bus
chug off to Baltimore, my classmates' palms
in rows of ghostly fog evaporating
off glass, one by one, like practice kisses
from an arm. I couldn't tell if their glee
was for Hayden's symphony or just the ride
away from Sister Bernadette
who catechized at her desk, muttering
she had no charity for charity
tuition brats who lost their field trip fee
like rotten Hophni. I opened orange to smear
a sky of trumpet angels flamed alive.

Orphan Lights

Two Fathers packed us shivering
into the rectory's station wagon
where our stuttered breaths fogged
windows spider-webbed with frost.
I rubbed circles with my sleeve
to see the cemetery angel glisten
above a mound so fresh it wore
no weeds. We left streetlamps
hovering like rotten nectarines
to creep through Harmony
Estates, where all the strands
arched rainbows over doors
and bushes trimmed to orbs.
I liked the plain lights best—
shimmering against eggshell
shutters or spiraling on reindeer
frozen in their ready rear
for flight. Comet and Cupid
rang inside my head, repeating
like plastic mangers where
every weary Joseph bowed
before a swaddled blue cocoon.
Timothy, our newest boy, kept
glancing backward at the miles
and mound the darkness held
where his handprints starred dirt.
His face turned alabaster
each time a coughing fit

bent him like a shepherd.
I wondered if the Holy Spirit hid
among oxen, or sheep, or flew
from bulb to bulb, blessing each
porch's wreath ribbon and risen
house number tacked in brass
impossible to read inside the glow.

The Free and Reduced-Price Meals Program of Anne Arundel County Public Schools

Crofton, 1993

You say your mother pays ahead and point
at the Reebok Pumps your father bought
on clearance when you saw him last
month. You say the family doesn't trust
your Velcro wallet: Wolverine comics,
Big League Chew, dough burns a hole
in your pocket. You say your Walkman
is a real Walkman. You say your ballooning
hand-me-downs are from He Who Whales
your arms purple from the bunk
above, whose raven locks cascade
across his face like an Algonquin brave—
this make-believe brother who leaves
bumpkin sprinters panting
at county meets and gleams until
someone asks why he never picks you
up. You say you can't put down
Robinson Crusoe. You say Pearl,
the lunch lady, is a cruel bitch
who hocks loogies in the meatloaf.
You say you'll be the lookout
if anyone wants to spark one

in the handicap stall as long
as you can hit it too. You say forget
this slop. You say you ain't starved.
The iron in your bones fell from dead stars.

Seamus Heaney in Community College Summer School

We drowse in the purgatorial
classroom, blinds cranked closed
while YouTube bogs, stuttering
through The Troubles, the Celtic
Tiger, the word 'Ulster' snapped
at the teeth. Heaney heaps

four centuries on his New York crowd
as if racing against a tea kettle
squeal for the suits and gowns
who splash laughter at his puns
before resuming a silence
anxiously funereal. Can I blame

my nightshift nurses, single dads,
and high school wunderkinds
for their panoply of dozing off,
some with cracked algebra books
for pillows, their faces slatted
from the blinds' thin light, fierce

as a farrier's blade? As if on cue
the clip's recitation freezes
at the appointed time to stream

beyond the screen into the hallway's
brittle halogens, where phones
chirp with all the private news

my rule delayed. One cell's ding
could pass for the cretaceous
projector Sister Margaret kept
on her cart, which I wobbled
through the narrow center aisle
of my fourth grade class lethargic

from kickball sprints. My nervous hand
held the Cousteau stills of jellyfish
and coral reefs until the creaking
cassette intoned for me to turn
the shadowed room deeper
into my giddy brownnoser's dream

of power. Frozen, Heaney's
eyes hover closed, sunken under
tufty eyebrows. The pixelated
chasm of his mouth holds its line.
Three stories below, the lawn crew
roars their mowers down the quad.

Bomb Threats

1998

After the first three, I dillydallied
and spun my locker open for a jacket
before rejoining the cattle drive
beyond diamonds to the clay-clod field
where the girls' field hockey team
sprained ankles. On game days
they sat at lunch taking turns
sketching trapezoids and sickle moons
of eye-black on each other's cheeks.
Crouching, I'd drift into the galaxy
of cleat divots their last game left
while copying another stoner's algebra.
The allure of sneaking off to spark
a joint wore off. Fire trucks arrived
without sirens. In thigh-high socks
the warriors we called girls ran plays
with imaginary sticks, their breaths
like smoke risen from yearbooks
a killer burns before he loads his gun.

The Day after the Massacre

Their sprinting footsteps thudded down the hall
accompanied by teenage blasphemy
so loud it shook the glass in classroom doors
shut tight to keep our sleepy lectures safe.

I stumbled past my teetered office stacks
of composition essays that argued
all opposition claims were trussed with lies
to stand there, phone in hand, for reckoning.

Instead, I saw Miranda and Jose,
their thin and perfect bodies smashed against
the free speech board, a frenzied swirl of tongues
as if they sought to grind themselves into

one spit-slick animal in skinny jeans.
Sweaty, shaking, I faced the corridor.
Dust motes orbited shafts of autumn light
that streamed through squares of window glare

where the custodian glanced up to grin
and wave, nonchalantly polishing the sill.
For one more day, no skulking gunman lurched
to spray and consummate our wide-eyed fall.

III.

It Pays in Exposure

The emcee who mispronounced your name
stands nervously by the coffee pot adjusting
his watch, waiting for your audience of four
to grow. It doesn't. Ten minutes late,
you boom your thanks into the mic and plunge
into an elegy interrupted in its closing
stanza by an octogenarian who resembles
your Great Aunt Gladys, shrieking
from the rear row for you to raise your face
so she can read your lips. Just then you realize
your glasses are in the car. You decide
during your second poem to cut your ninth.
During your third you decide to cut
your eighth. As you offer an anecdote
to introduce your last, the student taking notes
for his extra credit report stands and zips
every section on his backpack before booting
the side door into sunlight. Afterwards
the platter of cheese looks like brains.
Your lone buyer says to pick any letter
you like and inscribe your book lovingly
to it. Before you click your pen he says
to make it out to Z. The emcee apologizes
for the maintenance guys whamming
like drunk gravediggers down the hall.
You say you didn't hear them. He begins
to purse his lips to form the word *crowd*
but swallows it instead. Great Aunt Gladys

shuffles over to announce she disagrees
that poetry is so tough because she wrote
a little gem over by the cheese and unlike
the one about your cousin's suicide it rhymes
which you'll hear if you listen closely now:

A Drought September

I wanted the bank agent to find me in pieces
down by our mailbox, just as the crows
came hopping back after the blast
like gossipers at a wake. We had paced

three weeks without rain. Each cabbage
was a kindergarten shoe charred
in a school fire. My wife begged all month
for me to telegram her rich uncle

in Columbus. She rocked, fretting needles
on the porch. Whenever a distant tractor
rumbled on a neighbor's hill
she'd shiver at the billowed lion-manes

of dust spun up by its wheels. Nothing
was paved then. No one thought to name
the numbered roads. My quail shotgun
was a Christmas gift I hunted with

once. Two shells clacked in my pocket
through clouds of gnats. The bank man
was due at four. I broke the chamber
and stared into its empty wells

when, echoing off the barn, a breeze
brought my youngest daughter's voice
from her knotted rope swing
singing *olly olly oxen free.*

Infant Refuge

Texas, 1958

Seven months without a gig. Odessa
can't tell the difference between August
and April. Bible-thumping DJs guess
the drought will last until the good Lord thrusts
his righteous lips beyond the clouds to gust
relief across the Gulf. Tiptoeing stairs,
Orbison dodges the glinting busted
bottles that shimmer in the spectral glare

of his apartment's single hallway light.
The night is licorice. More rendered fat
from the chicken plant writhes its stink inside
the only Cadillac for miles. The matte
scuffed Ramirez across his lap goes flat
when tuned against his hummed falsetto E.
Its month-old strings are nearly blown. The vats
downtown putresce each chord to smithereens

so the staticky radio lullabies
twin orthogonal slumps in bucket seats.
The Sears portrait of Roy's infant son glides
and skates across the dash in rammish breezes
through tinted windows' slits. A milkman glares
and peers, rapping his bottle cap at dawn:
Mister, you better get that gal in there
back home before her daddy knows she's gone.

A Midnight Drug Deal in the Parking Lot of Royal Oak Church Where the Roof Has Recently Collapsed

Umbilical star-lit hands
pass the severed olive wings
dollars make fluttering
through October. Two idiot deer
loiter, sniffing in the roadway.
Idling there, six miles
from home, I flash my brights
at their eyes, which shimmer
like a boy's panicked exhumation
of marbles from a kitten's grave.

Changing the Discount Movie Theater Marquee

She wobbles up her ladder with a pole
that suctions to each letter of the flop
and drops its title to a bucket down below.
It splats on either side, an alphabet
cascading on the lot. I cannot see her face,

this perfect ponytail balanced high
inside the dusk, precipitously
perched upon the top-most step labeled NOT
A STEP, its warning raised in high relief
from molded plastic. Cosmic splatters hid

such warnings on the twenty-footers we
leaned against those lakeside palaces
in Michigan, hungover and aloof,
to scrape away a century and caulk
the cracks inside each sill before a brush

could lick a coat, out-glistening the sun.
When my dizzy eyes looked down I felt
each meal I ever ate knock inside my throat.
On my fifteens I'd smoke uncomfortably
on docks, cross-legged, mindful of the edge.

But here, the orange of early evening falls
until a row on the marquee is free,
blank as plaster, and she, bold daughter
of the sunset, proceeds to fix the names
for reels that spin to burn away the dark.

Lines Overheard before a Faculty Meeting

There should be a big list of frogs.
Are they ready to join the workforce?
In the beginning, 23 states flailed
in the political wind. I can't tell
any of them apart. I'm talking about
the kind that live in trees. Maybe
they have a future in plumbing.
Theoretically, it starts in 3rd grade.
One monster, many tentacles.
The whole field put their heads
together. In a pile of deep shit.
Sometimes they sit there glowing.
They just have to endure a body
of assessments. The rumor is the law
won't allow you time to transition.
That clock gets us all to heaven.

Community College Office Hours

Cassie's poems don't look right
in my handwriting, he said,
but your class killed our printer.
She had a drawer you never saw.

I've been off dope six months now
and am trying to get the kids back
from her parents, who are
the worst sons of bitches on earth.

That's my boss texting me again.
Today, can you believe it, I threw out
the purple scissors that on nights
we hoped to make love high

she used to trim her pubic hair.

The Pornographer

Sometimes when I'm winding the orange
extension cord around my arm I hear them
chatting about the weather while they dress
down the hall. Once I heard weeping
and found my male lead, nude in a puddle
of tears and snot, lacing his boots
cross-legged on the floor, still hard.
This basement hears two thousand
species of moan. Each shoot's sheets
bleach whiter than poached tusks.
When my wife surrenders, snoring
inside her sleep mask, I slip inside
my laptop headphones to edit out
the whispered lines I fed, my easy
implausibilities no one can remember.

Trust Fall

Close your eyes and think of the porpoises
everyone but Marion loved when we swam
at our last retreat. The purpose here
is to hear what a soft breeze predicts
about next quarter's earnings, knowing
your brains won't splatter on the rocks
when you tip back into nothing. Something
is there. Someone's arms are out. I like
to think of those arms as the Holy Spirit
even if it's just our friends in accounting.
Can you imagine? They spend all day
making sure none of you embezzle
a hole punch. A few of them are getting
up there, so try to feel lighter. Maybe suck
in your holiday gut. Don't tally
all the cookies you regret. I'm looking
at you, Marion. No peeking. Not even
at the day moon working overtime
like a dateless intern. Can you smell
that honeysuckle? Another wonder
in nature's spreadsheet. It all rounds up
clean to zero. Surrender when I say go.

Clearance Tie

Red, like its stickered price
or the acne-cheeked boy who goes
stag to a church dance. Some nights
it's just us and the Holy Ghost, staring
at paper decorations. The spirit plots
a spider in every corner to make the worst
table worse. Thin blue webs meander
like veins—a suave touch for three
dollars and eighty-seven cents. Beneath
the department store vent it flutters
whenever the air kicks on, which is
our colloquial way of saying
indoors we try to forget glaciers
will soon be cubes for punch. Ugliness
always has a sister who dances right
under the disco ball to feel her skin silver
into scales. She smiles too much at mass
just to make a poor boy fidget
his hand-me-down tie. All he has
to do is look at her and die.

On a Newswire Photograph of Children Pretending to Build the Berlin Wall, 1961

They beam to watch each other disappear
behind mounting scraps. One stack teeters
into a pile. No matter. Gravity
doesn't stand a chance against their gloves. See
how sticks are tucked like rifles, pointed straight
at buttoned coats? A grin says bang and waits
for its brother's giggly death to fall
into grass no longer grass at all,
flat from boots and frost. What boy can convince
himself he's lost? The mortar gray of sky
bares no seraphim. Vengeance is a wince
he wears unwell. And so his turn to die
is another plot, glaring at the ones
he'll soon obliterate with bricks and guns.

IV.

Another Country

Some nights I return to the crickets
singing to my sickbed there
in my dead aunt's room. The concussion
migraine I earned losing a game
of chicken on my Huffy throbbed
through the damp cloth folded
on my brow. In my hair I felt
the asphalt's scrape, its drizzle-
damp pebbles and bits of glass.
My pulse pounded like oars
inside my ears each time I woke
to kick the sheet another country
away. Beyond the hall faintly
I heard the laughter of Gilman women,
ice rattling their glasses, endless
rounds of cards shuffled and dealt.
At eight, the pain was so immense I asked
the ceiling fan if I would see morning.
From time to time I flipped my cloth
to find the other side as volcanic
as I had left it. The distant kitchen light
pooled its wan puddle under the door.
Each time it stung my eyes I closed them.
I knew there were enough hands
out there to lift my body up.

The Crisfield Winter Consumptives of 1908

for Norman Dubie

Like mating grackles Toby's dungarees
fluttered from the window into snow.
From my sill I watched mother pitch
his bare room barer: three blankets,
sling shot, church shirt, and the stool
he carved with father that summer
before their chests began to rumble
like locomotives. It wobbled when
he stood by the wash bin, scrubbing
dirt from his chin. Each night I'd plant
a foot to hold it firm and make certain
he used soap. I'd spit to slick his cowlick,
though I knew five was much too old
for a sister to linger by like a nanny,
petting the scar behind his ear.
Dr. Wilson said he never saw a wound
so small need a stitch. (He arrived
the next morning, thin as a pitchfork
when the blizzard broke.) At dusk,
winded and bootless, mother limped
our good lamp out into flurries
and smashed its oily belly down
to burn those scattered coughs before
she fainted in the poverty of ashes.

The Houses of the Poor

here beyond the city pink
tufts of insulation flutter
past siding torn or broken
sprawling in tire-strewn
lawns where peeling porches
slant beneath the weight
of washers jutting always
open lids like dingy flags
here between two rivers
nestled among the ancient
oaks surrendering to stubble
fields the sharecroppers'
shacks disintegrating one
can drive past them slowly
on a Tuesday night hearing
the overlapping melancholy
of frogs in early spring
among mucky kingdoms
in drainage ditches full
of littered chip bags
floating in the moon's
radiant preoccupation where
croaks venerate each house's
harsh uncurtained light
strung as if on a strand
along this road give or take
twenty miles until a strip
of county beach we all

share in summer splashing
forthwith to save our neighbor's
bronze toddler stripped
down to her diaper reaching
to poke an opaque blob
its blossomed tentacles
pink and fanning nearer

Room to Room

It terrified us to know the world
drove past for hours—ratty couch,
muddy pile of shoes, the sepia
dead we loved in frames above
the reading chair—everything
visible from our mailbox, the door
blown open like a hospital gown.

We told ourselves the tumbler
never caught, our hands forgot—
keys, coffee, electric bill, our boys
clamoring for us to change
the batteries in their beeping
games we hated. Through the screen
I peered for the murderer, crouched

in some shadowed corner, imagining
how the authorities would recount
my suffering spelled in splatter
on the ceiling. *He fought for his life*
they always sigh into the camera before
the screen floods with the wreckage
of a body in photos mold-flecked

from years in storage, a sheet
draped over the frozen face.
From room to room I crept,
an umbrella clutched like Excalibur

while our puppy trailed, bewildered
and wagging. He ran donuts
as we carried in a trunk-load

of groceries, our great protector
whose stupid tongue panted dusk.
He gnawed a knotted sock to tatters
while we filled the pantry shelves
beneath our backyard garden beets,
arranged in rows by month, floating
like butchered organs in their jars.

House Hunters

Chad and Beatrice find three havens in the Outer Banks. Their price point is a half-mil, which their agent says should make them pragmatic in this market. She enunciates *prioritize* as if it was a species of endangered crane. The first cottage lacks a hot tub, outdoor shower, and beachfront walkway. Beatrice rolls her eyes breezing through each mauve room. She stands beneath the hand-carved plaque on its porch, "Makeshift Eden," and pretends to gag, poking at the fake puke in her mouth. A block away they find "Fancy Living." Its renovated kitchen shimmers like a morgue. All the cabinet pulls are brass. They mumble *marble countertops* and take turns waving their hands in front of the automatic faucet. Chad catches the flaw: there's only one bathroom. He scrunches his face. He can already imagine his daughter's toothpaste spittle flecked across the mirror and his in-law's stale wine farts. The final house is "Seaside Bliss," a sand-stilt mansion. Beatrice twirls through the foyer like a debutant understudy in the wings, giddy for her first curtain-call bouquet. She makes soft little squeals each time she opens a closet. Then the agent cracks the basement door. It's filled with unquenchable fire and demons. *Once a year the demons cry out for blood*, she intones, fingering her clipboard. Chad and Beatrice nod in solemn understanding. They ask if the demons adversely impact the foundational integrity, the resale value, if screams trail back upstairs after a body is thrown down. *All you have to do*, their agent reassures, *is gather up the clothes*. The camera zooms in on their relief. Chad says he'll call the bank and pull some strings. He says they'll make it work.

The Eviction

The crooked antlers of our neighbors' chairs
teeter mist-slick in a borrowed truck
that flattens out the afternoon each time
its bearings creak away another load.
It could have seated ten, the oval table
I never shared that props a pyramid
where upturned seats glisten palely without
stain darkening their slats. Listlessly
the mother tosses in her candlesticks,
which spill, tumbling, like oblong pinballs
pinging on the bed. The rain picks up
and runnels down my pane. Through its blur
I see six siblings climb and pass the twine
to bind their jumble like a ransomed child.

At the Women's Shelter

A stenciled Mickey Mouse adorned the wall.
He bent to hug a wheelchaired girl whose shirt
read *I'm Okay With Me.* Green peppermints
in handblown candy dishes sat throughout
on tables, countertops. A zoo in plush
nestled on my comforter — two frogs
peeked from the pouch of mother kangaroo.
They smelled heavenly, like those breezy springs
fabric softener bottles advertised
on rainbow shelves my family's cart pushed past.
The counselor smiled and said kids called her Nan.
I kicked her arms away and stayed inside
the shadow of my steamed-up Batman mask
beneath my cot because I was a bruise.

During the Seventh Inning Stretch, a Country Time Lemonade Commercial Airs

Wherein our bearded father,
flannel-clad, grins into the camera,
reaching out to us before
we're transported suddenly
to a dappled mossy hollow
where none of our three siblings
frolicking in slow-mo trip
on the gnarled witch-finger roots
beneath a canopy of willows.
The lake's emerald skin ripples
by a rope swing swaying
to a guitar's shimmered arpeggios,
louder now and echo-drenched
as if plucked by an inconsolable
alpine shepherd mourning
his runt lamb that tumbled red
across the crags. Our mother
is a blond soundless laugh —
her brief flash of teeth flares
the lens. When the camera pans,
our tiny hands are clutching
the rope's lowest knot. The pitcher
brimmed with lemonade sweats
fistfuls of ice to puddles
on an immaculate stump wreathed
in ivy. The glass is empty.

Cartoon Network Airs Nine Commercials Straight

for my son Graham

a school of chromis flashing
aquamarine   this slippage across
smudged glasses   each demand

swims inside his little face

gargantuan cheeseburgers
dripping their speckled mystery
toxin   toy drones floating

above fenced grins   flamingo-pink
arrows a horde of girls
arc inside a treehouse etcetera

he is waiting for his bears
to come back singing   oblivious

that the scrunched credits rolled
beneath cop cruisers sirening
cardboard apartments down

his beckoned name passes
innocuously as a moth

so when another theme starts
after glow shoes   water balloons
competing brands of bike & the high

squeal from a whistling football
he bites a pretzel into wings
& flies it to our darkened hall

where his pretend lasers chirp
incessantly until some enemy

emerges desperate out of nothing

Amplitude

for Bruce Bond

I tune my son's guitar to open D
and let him strum one major chord, his nose
pressed against the porch's snow-flecked pane
so he can belt his morning song at wrens

who find we're out of seed again. *Spin spin*
my decision machine is how his chorus
goes, a child's exercise in consonance
that drones his nickel strings ringing flat.

Pom-Pom was the tribal nickname for
the Maxim gun and its one-pound shell,
my book explains, which the British leveled
against South Africa in the Second

Boer War. I cringe and try to skip
the glossy panoramic gray of gaunt
armies rotting on the savannah — one boy
small as mine whose open eyes seem to stare

at vultures circling above him though
I know it is an accident of space.
The Scottish baron Sir Mackinnon said
the Maxim would prove to be *a great*

peace-preserver. Our local weatherman
forecasts slush all day, good snowball stuff,
back and forth from snow to freezing rain
through midnight. When my son drops his pick

inside the belly of his Schoenhut,
one-third the size of my own acoustic,
he crouches on his knees and shakes it
upside down so gravity can work

its law, which rattles like the bullet
a surgeon's forceps ping inside a pan
so he can show the nurses, whose relief
unties the knotted ribbons of their masks.

Poem Written One-Handed While Holding a Newborn in My Arms

for my son Roan

Four bouquets explode
atop the hospital sill
where closed blinds
smuggle in tiny coos
of sunbeam. My wife's
robotic bed adjusts
beneath her fitful sleep,
softly whirring. Soon
the nurse will knock,
young and giddy to ruin
our dim den with light.
Until then, little fox,
your bloodshot eyes
and mine can watch
another rerun gameshow
soundless in the corner:
Farrah Fawcett hair,
plaid lapels and paneled
station wagons glistening
in showroom glare.
On mute it's hard to tell
which contestants win.
They weep no matter what.

V.

Here Lies a Patriot

Some nights I dream I take a bullet
for the president. My convalescent bed
snaked with tubes and wires beams
into every American home. He looms,
hand on pillow, thanking my mother
for tending valor like a seed.
Trembling in the corner, she clutches
a Secret Service handkerchief,
her pride wider than Montana.
The incessant click of cameras
sounds like an orphanage learning
how to tap dance. Three dressings
of gauze cover the hole in my chest,
which he peels away to bury
a long stem in the gash. *Daisies*
always were my favorite, he says
with a wink, before his entourage
squeaks through the corridor. Alone,
weeping down my open gown,
I behold at last the majesty
of my bequest, prim and sprouting
from its soft red vase, wishing finally
I had more wounds to fill.

Four Failed Elegies for Alexander Hamilton

I.

little bastard genius America
land of westward handshakes
knee-jerk test-prep land
of newborns shrieking tossed
in ghetto dumpsters (where
hark the gunfire blooms
the city night's orgasm) my
land reduced to stockpiles
at least we grant your face
more purchase power than
the redhead rapist gracing
the defunct $2 the only bill
I horded in a Jif jar under
my bed the summer I felt
my skin begin to ______.

II.

vault-stalkers speculators assholes
your tribe wrecked the skyline
milkshakes even the taste & smell
of rivers etcetera I wonder

deep down didn't you loathe
the way they grinned & shook
your hand limply speaking always
to the crown of your scalp

III.

your mother Rachel spreads her Nevis legs like dawn

IV.

& Burr despicable rowing
through the dawn fog
from Weehawken as his lead
pinballs around your ribs

rowing as he lisps the eight
names of your children yes
having seen them sprout
in & out of waistcoats

while Pendleton diminished
to a hazy speck collects
your gilded pistols (hastily
cocooned in silk) & this finally

the sum ledger: your guts
leaking out beneath
the massive limb blasted where
you threw away your fire

The Sons and Daughters of Unimpeachable Light

We planted lilies in our chamber pots
and watched them bloom October
in the heated greenhouse. After rains
we nursed our brandies there,
voyeurs among the greasy kingdom
of slugs. No skein of fog could ravel
our spirits — we were the sons
and daughters of unimpeachable light,
free from creaking wheels
of carriages, the city's devastating
stench, the rats who bobbed on bones
in gutter currents. Once a month
we granted audience to ruddy serfs
whose babes refused to suck, who woke
at dawn to gawk at maggots wreathed
around a heifer's anus. Each turd
we called *dear sir*. They'd slouch
and fret and spin their hats awaiting
wonderwork. *How dreadful*, we said,
passing chalices brimmed with sorbet.
We recited sympathies. We raised
our rubied fists to brace our yawns.

Manifest Destiny: Utah Gift Shop Postcard, 1876

The foppish engineer has posed before —
coattails fanned, contrapposto as a whore.
Sun glints the droopy U his watch chain makes
dangling at his belt. This is his rightful place,
he thinks, beside three Chinese laborers
morose and half-asleep. They don't confer
but stand on their railway handcar, unfazed
their tracks bolt down the desert's throat. The haze
beyond is craggy scrub and shadscale wilt.
The shortest worker winces back. He's built
so far across the western sand he's cured
himself of hope. The stoner clerk demurred
when I said what the hell. I was his last.
I broke his dream inside the counter glass.

Election Night

for Thomas McGrath

Snow cauls the gaped maws
of trenches. I haunt my couch
rooting for demons.

The Devouring

Goya, "Saturn Devouring His Son," c. 1819 – 1823

1.

seventy-three deaf teetering
on chairs his dining room
blacker than a consumptive
lung Goya nightmared

Saturn furring indefinite
space the hands biting
his son's spine crippled
me in the rear row of Mazow's

lecture as he clicked
the carousel let us
not dwell he said
on the late master's late

horrors brilliant as they are

beside me a sorority
pledge plucked hairs
from her brush before
she twirled the living

strands knotless weightless
around a finger their brittle
ends she smothered between
lips shimmering balm

2.

Jesus my father muttered
through his potatoes I should
turn this nature shit off

reddened frantic pumping the last
ocelot paw disappeared
inside an unhinged jaw

the next morning three
lunch tables end to end the nuns
assembled for the massive sprawl

of boa constrictor come lay
your hands children on its scales
the zoo guide said you will find them

surprisingly dry to the touch
the school save one a queue
writhing against the wall

Adam this is not Genesis
Sister Theresa said frowning my
heavens it cannot speak

3.

can I say now how my teeth
that final drunken June
vised each night a throb

that woke into a lurching
stagger like the frog
my dull mower blades

scalped the breeze licking
the pink of his dim doomed
brain I gawked hungover

little pulse little pulse
for some seconds beatific
his halo burning sunlight

4.

Goya's vision a madness of eyes
wide as sink drains unstoppered

is it Saturn Spain gruesomest
himself   gnawing the mangled
stump his son's left arm

four syllables *re-*
mem-ber-ance the priest would
mispronounce his wafer
aloft the abstract
deliverance of a torso

later I held my pillow above
my head the way my glistening
hero raised his garish
belt Byzantine inside the ring

where some loser
masked unmasked I cannot remember

his face unconscious bled
beside the folding chair that held
the form his bashing gave

5.

parched their bearded
father stoops delirious
squinting for drones

raping clouds again names
of friends blister between
his toes he has outlived

everything but the taste
of his sons' hair when gently
he kisses them incessantly

at the altar of their sleep
though they swat his whiskers
back to shadows pacing

6.

listen my uncle said why
Rwanda why peck this
extra credit shit instead of

an extra shift scrubbing
dishes for a car your girlfriend
isn't going to drive your ass around
forever why at fifteen he said I
rebuilt engines blindfolded

he tapped my monstrous
monitor this was the nineties

our decade of quaint impeachment

if you had any brains at all
he said you would realize those
people over there have slaughtered
each other for centuries grinning
as if for emphasis he left
his pointer finger mashed
on the backspace my blurred
cursor a machete hacking
silence into itself

7.

Trump duck-faced pouting
shrugs and says he needs
time to research the Klan
like they are a parasite
no upright citizen discusses
without first reading how
they latch lay eggs
build their little white

colonies inside the colon I'll
understand my student signs
to her interpreter if now
I can't make up the quiz but
they kept flicking my ears
three white boys kept flicking
my ears in the parking lot
so I'd stop walking and look
up at the confederate
flag there strung
in their truck cab hanging

8.

it is not a boy Saturn eats
legs buttocks biceps fully

formed frozen muscular
nakedness this manhood is

a terrible price to pay for being
born one morning

delirious with fever I heard
my eldest sobbing

again his dead grandfather
had died inside his dream

and though I held him so
close his tears and snot pasted

on my shirt I could not gather
the strength to lift him up

9.

it passes into family lore the hunger
of a Vermont farm boy thrashing
in that fitful dreamless
Depression-era sleep his belly

rationed to ribs two handfuls
of popcorn his blizzard
dinner after shoveling
the barn path milking another
frigid monotony of pails

a Sopwith mobile spins
above his gaunt face
stubble-chinned that blitzkrieg
decade later plummeting

twenty-four thousand feet dear god

when drowsy medics pace
from face to face and find
the whole crew obliterated

how they marvel at the ghost
trapped inside him still
pelvis left leg shattered
no pulse no pulse until
they see the death sheet breathe

10.

let us go then you and I
down the cavernous
red throat echoing

down past epiglottis
our patient etherized
upon the table we will make

a human chain to the belly
we can hoist one morsel
tattered dripping inchoate

this memory of August
burning the White
House burning Dolly Madison

her carriage flees with silver urns
but the slaves Sioussat
McGraw and Jennings fifteen

years old find a ladder
and brace it up against
the plaster's cannon-quakes

to trim our father's portrait
from its frame while
drunken redcoat torches

somersault through
windows the capital a body
shrieking on its pyre

unfree they free his gaze
together terrorized straining
pilgrims in the blaze

Nero's Torches

after Henryk Siemiradzki's painting "Nero's Torches," c. 1876

The revelers who come to watch Christians burn
are bored with suffering before the stakes are lit.
Partially disrobed, one courtesan resists the urge
to masturbate while the centurion behind her
ogles her rump. No figs or olives glisten yet
where chalices scoop the sun, where three senators
exchange hushed belated dreams of treason
not far from Nero's bed, shimmering and borne
by a troupe of Africans who have perfected
swallowing their rage. Caesar's rigid tiger glares
from the palace patio at those faithful, bound
with tinder, their stakes spiral-garlanded like posts
for a wedding tent. Two workers stoke the brazier
into an orange confusion. Others climb ladders
to tack mocking crosses on the woven bundles
cocooning each body. Momentarily a torch
will make a torch of each who thought mistakenly
that Rome could tolerate itself. Four censers
billow on pillars, anticipating the stench
of fat liquefied by flames. The feast awaits.

The Author

Adam Tavel is the author of six books of poetry, most recently *Rubble Square* (Stephen F. Austin State University Press, 2022).

www.ingramcontent.com/pod-product-compliance
Lightning Source LLC
Chambersburg PA
CBHW030428310726
48979CB00009B/1663/J

* 9 7 8 1 9 3 9 5 7 4 3 5 0 *